The Path to Coaching Mastery

How to coach people for interviews, work and business.

Daniel Mokades

DEDICATION

I would never have been able to do all the coaching I have done without the help of three remarkable people.

Anna Burgess
Kura Dione-Warren
Raphael Mokades

Thank you for your patience, kindness, support and belief. Thank you for giving me the chance to get really good at something.

This book is dedicated to you.

Contents

Daniel Mokades

.

ALSO BY DANIEL MOKADES

Conflict: Part one of the Master Smith cycle
Catalyst: Part two of the Master Smith cycle
Funny Ting

The path to coaching mastery

Hello.

This is a book about coaching. In fact, it's a book about the path to getting really good at coaching.

I think I'm a pretty good coach, which is why I'm qualified to write this book. I wish I could tell you that this was a natural gift, that I emerged from the womb with this magical ability to help others, but it's not true. The reason I'm a good coach is that I've done a lot of coaching. At the time of writing, I've done about fifteen thousand hours of it. During these sessions, I've made lots of coaching mistakes.

Really—lots. Some of them were appalling.

That is why I am now a good coach.

One of the great things about doing something a lot—an awful lot—is that you learn from it. The more open your attitude is, and the more you can shrink your ego and learn from your mistakes, the better you will become.

1

If you're reading this book, then you probably want to become better at coaching too. I hope that this book will help you (that was certainly my intention in writing it), but I also hope that you will be brave. I hope that you will take action and try lots of things and make lots of mistakes, and try to learn from them. That is the most assured path to coaching mastery.

Let's begin, shall we?

Part One - What is Coaching?

It's a muddy picture, this one. Coaching means lots of different things to lots of different people. I'm not going to try and capture all of those things here. That would be silly, and I save my silliness for weekends and Las Vegas.

Instead, let me tell you what I mean by coaching, specifically in the context of this book.

I'm talking about helping people—especially students and graduates—to pass job interviews and assessment processes. As a shorthand, let's call this **interview coaching**. This is the bulk of the coaching that I have done in my career.

I'm also talking about coaching people in their careers as they try to navigate the workplace advance, learn, earn more money and get better at whatever it is that they do. Let's call this **business coaching**.

Lastly, I'm talking about coaching people in your immediate work environment. That will often mean people who work for you, or report to you. Sometimes however, it can mean coaching a colleague, a friend, or (less commonly) a boss. Let's call this **workplace coaching**.

There is one other person that I want to talk about coaching: yourself. Yes, you can coach yourself. If you have ever psyched yourself up for an onerous task, then that is just what you have done. This is **self-coaching**.

This book is not designed to show a complete novice how to coach. Nor is it a self-help book or a guide to therapy or helping people who are seriously unwell. When I talk about coaching, I am talking about one or more of those four things.

Rapport

It's bloody hard to coach someone if you don't like them. It's almost impossible to coach them if they don't like you. One thing I tell coaches is that a piece of coaching is useful *only if the client finds it so*.

The inverse is also true; if a client finds a session unhelpful, *then it has been unhelpful*.

If you want to coach people, then you need to remember this. It's very important. When I like you, and you like me, and we're getting along, we have rapport.

Rapport is at the very centre of coaching mastery.

Building rapport

The best way that I know of to build rapport with people is to be genuinely interested in them and genuinely interested in helping them.

This means listening.

Listening is the master skill, the ultimate habit, of a skilled coach. This habit—the habit of being *genuinely interested* in others and truly listening to them—is something that most of us already have to some degree or another. Think about a famous person whom you admire. Now imagine yourself coaching them. It's hard to see how you wouldn't be genuinely interested in listening to them. You would want to know about their hopes, their dreams, their fears and their challenges. And you would want to help.

We all have the ability to listen, but some of us listen more, or to a deeper level, than others.

The important thing is to try and activate this muscle and ramp it up during a coaching session. I suggest that you approach a coaching interaction with two thoughts:

1. This person has something to teach me.
2. I will try to suspend my judgement of them as a person during this session.

While we all have people whom we especially enjoy coaching, I try to establish a baseline of interest in everyone who I work with. This is basic professionalism for a coach. It will bolster your ability to coach the widest possible range of people, and to help them achieve real results.

In addition to activating your genuine interest in a participant, there are other qualities which help in building rapport.

Charisma helps, though it is not essential.

Natural authority helps too, though it is not essential.

Being a person whom others want to be around (a radiator, not a drain) also helps.

So does having a big toolbox (more on this later), range and depth of coaching experience, working in an environment conducive to coaching, being positioned as an expert, being well-dressed and acting with confidence and kindness from the moment you meet someone.

All of these things help, but all of us have limitations. So what's the best approach?

Work with what you've got.

Are you tall? Great. Use it[1].

Do you have a voice like honey poured over thunder? Marvellous. Use it.

Do you dress well and wear a delightful fragrance? Is the pace at which you speak fast or slow? Do you speak softly or loudly? Do you gesticulate a lot or a little? All these things feed into building rapport. Some of them are beyond your control. Others are not. Consider them, and consider which is the most *potent* you, the one most people would *want* to be coached by.

A coaching master can turn up in a hoodie with food stains on it, looking a little the worse for wear after a long night, and, so long as he has genuine interest in his client, listens to them, and has some decent tools he can still do a useful job. He will start with the odds stacked against him, however.

---

[1] There are numerous studies showing the correlation between height and success in all sorts of areas. Perhaps the most striking example is from *Blink* by Malcolm Gladwell. In the U.S. population, about 14.5% of all men are six feet or over. Among CEOs of Fortune 500 companies, that number is 58%.

For the most part, I suggest you try to look the part and act the part, at least until you truly *become* the part.

At that point, feel free to chuck on a pair of slippers.

Calibration

There are several meanings for this word. For now, this is the one I'm interested in:

Carefully assess, set, or adjust (something)

The "something" is the person you are coaching. The "assess" bit is figuring them out. Calibration can be an elusive process, but it's a bloody important one. If you dive in and try to coach everyone in the same way, then your results will be very patchy. I've seen coaches who do this. They have their script, they have their habits and patterns, and they use them unfailingly with each person. The result is that they have clients who are "clever," who "listen," and whom they "like." They also have clients who are "shit," who "don't listen," and whom they despise.

The clients aren't shit, of course. The coach is, or rather they are not calibrating. Coaches who don't calibrate can be very good for clients who fall within their coaching "comfort zone". They are not on the path to coaching mastery though, because there are a significant number of people whom they cannot help, and who they might in fact hinder.

How to calibrate

From the very first moment you encounter a client, whether in person, on the phone or on video, you need to be listening and watching *intently*. The more time you spend doing this, the richer the detail you will collect, and the finer your calibration will become. When I meet somebody for the first time, here are some of the things I try to notice:

How much warmth do they greet me with? Where are they on a spectrum of emotional demonstrativeness? Are they more physically expressive or more closed?

Are they a fast or slow speaker? Do they breathe slowly and evenly or the opposite?

What are they wearing? Have they taken any noticeable care in preparing for this session with me?

What is their background? Class, race, religion? Can I make an educated guess from their full name or how they speak?

How old are they?

Are they carrying anything?

How prepared are they? Some clients arrive with a fat sheaf of notes. Others cannot find my office.

Are they late, early or just on time? If they're early, then how early? When they arrive, how do they interact with the person that greets them?

How's their handshake? How's their eye contact? What's their blink rate like? Do they appear tired or stressed?

What's their accent like? Can I place it?

As I begin to interact with the person, the information that I'm taking in begins to broaden and deepen:

When we sit down, which seat do they choose? How do they sit? What posture do they assume? Do they lean forward? Is their body language open or closed? Are they showing barrier signals?[2]

How do they respond to me? Do they want to control the flow of the conversation? Do they want to lead the interaction?

The answers to these questions—the information that a person gives you—should guide your coaching session.

You will notice of course, that I haven't asked them a single question about what they need coaching *for*. Not yet.

Calibration is about assessing who the person is, what sorts of qualities are native to them, and what type of state they are in on that particular day. It begins from the moment your client appears, and it continues throughout the session as you adjust and readjust to how things develop.

But calibration is just half of the story.

---

[2] Barrier signals are just the tip of the iceberg. If you want to be skilled at calibration, then you need to pay close attention to body language and to deciphering it. *Peoplewatching: The Desmond Morris Guide to Body Language* is the best book I have found on the subject. I also recommend watching *Big Brother*. (I'm not kidding.)

Flexing your style

I was doing some coaching for a police force. The objective was to help more junior officers to advance in their careers. One chap walked in and I'll never forget my interaction with him. He strode forward to greet me and thrust out his hand. His handshake was fierce.

"Daniel, is it? Very good, shall we sit over there? Right then. Let me tell you what I need. My interactions with people are very good—superb really—I know all the tricks to handling people efficiently, my issue is just the stupid assessment process and the role-plays especially."

"Ok, is—"

"The issue—let me tell you what it is, right—the issue, is that if these were real situations, then I would do really well. As I say, on the street, I'm totally in charge of a situation like that. Now, I've done this process twice and I keep getting rejected because of the bloody role-plays. So I need you to tell me how to pass them. The mark scheme and things. That's what I need to nail. That's the issue."

On another occasion, I was working with candidates applying for the Civil Service Fast Stream. My client buzzed the intercom and I struggled to hear her. When she came into the office, she inched the door open and peeked around it. Her first words were, "Um, sorry..."

As I greeted her, I saw that her shoulders were slumped, and although she was taller than me, she stooped and hunched as if trying to make herself smaller. She began our session by telling me that she was bad at interviews, terrified of making mistakes in them, and too nervous to do anything but stutter out idiotic answers to the interviewers' questions. She barely looked at me as she was telling me these things.

"How many interviews have you had?" I asked.

"Two," she replied.

"And how did you get on?"

"Awful. They were really bad."

"So, you didn't pass?"

"Well, no—I passed one—but I failed the other one. And I didn't do well in either of them."

Let's call these candidates Tom and Jean. If I used the same approach with both clients, what do you think results would be like?

Not very good. I agree.

Flexing your style is essential if you want to be a good coach. Sometimes, the nature of your client makes it obvious how you should adapt. To help Tom, I needed to take a more assertive and challenging approach. To help Jean, I needed to give some positive reassurance and guide her towards building her confidence and self-belief.

This is only a surface reading though. In fact, to help Tom, I needed to challenge him—yes—but I also needed to help him to build his self-awareness. To help Jean, I needed to challenge her belief (a very confident and powerful belief, in fact) that she was bad at interviews. Both clients needed to change their thinking to achieve their aims.

To be a really effective coach, you need to have the capacity to behave in different ways with different clients. Sometimes you need to challenge them. Sometimes you need to reassure them. Often, you need to do both. The more skilled your calibration becomes, the better you will get at flexing your style. The two processes are part of one system.

This being a book about coaching, I should probably insert a simple diagram with the words **CALIBRATE** and **FLEX** joined by two half-circular arrows. I think it would probably be more useful however, if you drew this diagram yourself. You're more likely to remember it if it's your own work. Here's some blank space for you.

It's worth pausing here to ask yourself a question: who would you prefer to coach, Tom or Jean? Whoever you pick can help you to identify your own more natural, comfortable coaching style. You can then start to recognize the sorts of clients whom you might find harder to coach.

Flexing with effect

At its core, flexing your style means doing something—anything—differently from how you normally do it. Let's look at an example.

I was observing a coach who worked professionally as a judge. During three sessions, I saw her use the same technique to teach debating basics. She would verbally list a series of options, and have her client write them down and repeat them back to her. During the latter part of the session, they applied what she'd taught them in an exercise. With the first two clients, this approach seemed to work well.

The third client was different. He became flustered and red-faced, and struggled to work the technique into his response to her questions. When the session was over, I gave her some feedback and a suggestion. The technique she was describing consisted of four separate parts. "Why don't you try this," I said, "have the client write down the parts in bold letters on four different coloured sheets of paper. Then ask them to stick them up in four corners of the room. You can then gesture to the corners to guide them through the technique or even ask them to go and stand in the different corners as they make their argument."

She tried the technique with her next client and it worked well.

The point here is not that what she was doing was wrong. It wasn't. It was working well for some of her clients. It was merely limited. By using a different approach (non-verbal, using space and movement), to communicate her technique the coach expanded her options. She added another tool to her toolbox.

Skilled language teachers are expert at this. When their learner encounters a new word, they will typically:

- Demonstrate the word in context and elicit (more on this later) its meaning from the learner.
- Highlight its relationship to other words or pieces of knowledge that the learner is familiar with.
- Write it out for the learner to see and to copy down.
- Say it, and have the learner repeat it back to them.
- Have the learner use the word in context, often in an exercise.

That is the essence of flexing your style; having different coaching options, techniques and tools to help your client. You'll use some approaches more often than others, just as a workman will use some tools more than others. The more tools you have, the more problems you can help to solve.

Below are some of the main tools which I find useful for achieving greater flexibility in my coaching. This is by no means an exhaustive list; as a coach you should continue to learn from different sources, to experiment and to find different methods that can work for your clients.

Technique: Reassure

This is a spectrum technique in depth and range. By *depth*, I mean that some clients will need a lot of reassurance, some a little, some none at all. You may find it helpful to mentally employ a ten-point scale for this technique.

By spectrum of *range*, I mean that some clients will need reassurance on some areas, ("Your knowledge on this issue is very clear to me", "It's okay to be nervous", "The situation you've described sounds brutal—you're handling it as well as anyone") but not on others. This might seem like an obvious point, but it's important to identify exactly which areas a client needs reassurance in. With Jean, for example, she needed deep reassurance on a few things, but she also needed challenging on some of her beliefs.

Technique: Build confidence

Building confidence is embedded in many of the other techniques that a skilled coach employs. That said, there is also great value for some clients in taking a direct approach.

There are lots of different methods dedicated to this subject and I will not try to list them all here. Instead, here are some of the things that I say to clients which tend to work well.

"I think you would make an excellent lawyer."
This is a very straightforward affirmation and I use it frequently. You can, of course, substitute "lawyer" for a different profession, or a different word, ("manager" for example). For this to work effectively you must believe what you are saying.

"Why do you think they have called you to interview? Is it because they feel sorry for you? Is it because you have a cool haircut? Absolutely not. I agree. It's because you're someone they might want to hire. They don't give out interviews for fun, do they?"
There is an obvious element of [playful] challenge embedded in this sort of statement. I find it especially useful in helping to redirect a client's thinking. This is useful for a client suffering from Imposter Syndrome.

"I want you to remember that you have earned your place at that interview just as every other person there has."
There is a strong affirmation embedded in this statement. There is also a second part which reminds the client that they are not alone at interview with some giant spotlight of scrutiny shining down upon them; there are many other people in the same situation.

"Standing behind you, there are twenty people who didn't get to the assessment centre. Standing behind them are another hundred who didn't get to the first interview. You have already done well to get this

far."

This construction serves to remind the client of how much they have achieved already. This must be delivered with care; if it's done clunkily it could make a client more nervous about the assessment centre. To avoid this, I might add a coda or rephrase things slightly: *"Don't worry about this bit! Forget about it! You've got to this point already—that's great. You should feel proud of what you've achieved. Keep getting to interview and you WILL get something good."*

"Do you think that you would make a good analyst? Do you know your stuff? I agree. Remember that please. Have some confidence in your abilities."

There is a note of challenge here again. Interestingly, I have never had a client say "no" to these questions. They might qualify their answers a bit ("I think so…") but that's all. When there is a lack of confidence for clients in interview situations, it does not seem to stem from doubts about their ability to do the job.

"Listen, I've read your CV, and from where I'm sitting, it's pretty fucking impressive."

The swearing here is important. It's there to shock the client and make them really sit up and take notice of the message. As with all of these messages, you must adapt them to suit your own personality. For a line like this to be effective, it's essential to deliver it congruently. What works for me might not work for you.

"I think you're a star, but what do I know? I'm just a coach."

The first part of this is straightforward: you're special, rare, powerful, bright. I struggle to analyse the second part however. I know that it works for me, but I'm not sure why. Perhaps it's the playfulness.

"I don't think you really know how good you are, so let me tell you."

Another statement with an element of challenge—a softer one this time. The second part isn't always necessary. Sometimes it's enough to shake my head and indicate my own surprise at my client's lack of confidence.

"That was a fantastic answer. I especially liked X and Y. Don't change a thing. Do that."
This is a particular powerful technique because it gives the client something specific to base their confidence on. When you mix this with careful criticism of other answers, it can really help the client to raise their overall confidence level.

From these examples, you can see that I like to use a mixture of praise, encouragement and challenge to directly build confidence. From time-to-time, I will also employ certain exercises such as The Confidence Number Line and The Arrow of Attention. I explain these in the resources section.

Technique: Set aspiration

"What do you want to focus on specifically in this session?" "What's the goal you want to achieve?" "What's the outcome you are looking for?" "Can we break this down into some smaller pieces?"

Questions like this can help you and your client to pin down exactly what they want from a session. They are also important in chunking down bigger goals into more manageable, individual aims.

For some clients, this can be the most helpful part of a session; a skilled coach helping them to articulate a precise aim. After all, the first step to catching a tiger is knowing what it looks like. We will return to this in The Mokades Method.

Technique: Challenge

Challenge comes in many forms. I visualize it less as a force against a force and more as a nudge on the arm and a redirection of energy; a "Have you considered this?" type of approach.

In Tom's case, I needed to challenge him, but I had to do it in a way that circumnavigated his possible resistance.

This was tricky.

Tom was making certain assumptions:

"My issue is just the **stupid assessment process** and the role-plays especially...I keep getting rejected because of the bloody role-plays...So I **need you to tell me how to pass them**. The **mark scheme** and things. That's what I need to nail. **That's the issue.**"

His goals were clear—he wanted to pass the role-plays—but his assumptions were limiting his ability to change his approach. He was stuck in a rut.

It struck me that Tom's main issue was that he didn't listen. More than that, he didn't seem to realize the value of listening or of being seen to listen.

To challenge Tom effectively, I needed to help him to recognize that he wasn't really listening. We ran a practice role-play, and every time Tom showed that he hadn't been listening, I would pause the role-play and ask him what the speaker had said. He'd paraphrase. I would challenge him on it—strongly.

"What *exactly* did she say, Tom? You need to listen, and you need to *signal* that you're listening. This is massive in the **mark scheme**. That's the **goal you set**, remember. Come on, mate! You can do this. Concentrate."

When Tom left the session, I asked him what he needed to focus on.

"Listening!" he announced.

"And?"

"*Show* that I'm listening. Write stuff down. Use their words. Summarize what they've said to me."

In short, I didn't try to challenge Tom directly on his lack of self-awareness or on his claims about his people skills. Instead, I linked *his* goal to the area that he needed to be challenged on: his listening.

Technique: Use past history

This is what I did with Jean when she told me that she was bad at interviews. I used her past history to show that this wasn't the case.

"So, these interviews you had before, Jean...Let's just back up for a moment. You said you did badly in both, but you passed one. How does that work? Were they just feeling generous? How did you pass if you didn't do well?"

After some back and forth, Jean began to disentangle her general fear of interviews from the two specific outcomes (one pass, one fail) that she had experienced. She slowly came to accept the idea that she had, in fact, done well in one of the interviews. Not perfectly, of course. But well enough to get through. From there, the door was open to help her begin to shift her central belief that she was "bad" at interviews. Specifically, I helped her get to the point where she was basing her belief about giving a good interview more on her ability to do the job and her proven skills than anything else.

Let's suppose for a moment that Jean had said this:

"I've had seven interviews, and I've failed all of them. I'm really bad at interviews."

What might your approach be in this case? There are different ways you might try to tackle this, but I suggest you don't avoid past history; it's valuable information and can help you in flexing your approach. If Jean had said the above, I would first dig a little deeper. I would ask when she'd had these interviews, if she'd received feedback, if she agreed with it, if she'd identified any trends herself. "I'm bad at interviews," is pretty vague. "I struggle with nerves," or, "I think I need to develop my commercial awareness," is far more helpful for a coach. If a client gives me the former sort of statement, then I might say something like, "Well, let's just try a few practice questions and see if we can figure out what you need to work on."

If they are more attuned to their development area[s] then I might say, "Well, that's very helpful. It sounds like we've got a clear idea of what we need to work on today."

Whatever a client's past history is, you, and they, can use it. Experience, and the ability to reflect on that experience, is an essential component of learning.

Technique: Use anecdotes

Stories are a wonderful way to help a client. They can bypass potential resistance, and for some clients they connect far better than more direct feedback methods.

Overtly, a coach can use them to amplify themes or to offer [alternative] scripts which are helpful for the client. For coaches interested in Neuro-Linguistic Programming, you may want to read more about the Milton Method or Analog Marking. Simply put, these techniques allow a coach to smuggle in suggestions as embedded hypnotic commands.

Here are some examples:

SCRIPT A – *You are not alone*

"Do you know, it's funny that you mention nerves, because I was catching up with a guy called Karim yesterday and he used to suffer from the most awful nerves, he really did. Hands shaking, bad eye contact, stuttering—the lot. He'd interviewed with a whole load of law firms before I saw him, and he really didn't know what to do. Then we did the exercise I've just showed you—the Arrow of Attention—and it really worked for him. He didn't get the first one, but he got offers from the following two. It really can make a difference. Practice it tonight and let me know how you get on. It's a gradual process, you know…"

SCRIPT B – *politeness costs nothing, rudeness costs a fortune*

"This will interest you. There was a company I was doing some work for, and the Chief Engineer told me this story about an applicant. The girl comes in, does well on all the tests—really smashes the coding exercise. Then she has the interviews; she's great, really good answers. Scores highly across the board. Then, just as she was leaving, she needed to collect her coat from reception. Now, as she collected it, apparently, she was quite rude to the receptionist. She was on her phone and was just quite short with her. Anyway, the receptionist told the Chief Engineer and they didn't hire her because of it. Such a silly thing to do, right?"

SCRIPT C – *aligning confidence with competence*

"A friend of mine told me a story about these two graduates he hired. One of them was really charming and when she first started, she got on with everyone. The other one was quieter, more reserved. Took her a lot longer to find her feet. But once they got a few months in, the real picture emerged. Turns out that the charming girl's work wasn't that good. She was slow, and she kept making mistakes. When people gave her feedback she got pissed off, and so they started giving her feedback less often. The other girl though—her work was stellar. Really good standard, and she worked fast. When the probation period came to an end they didn't retain the first girl. The second one is still there now, three years in, and she's the youngest ever manager they have. Competence matters."

SCRIPT D – *using analog marking*

"I remember my first proper DJ gig, you know? It was in this awful, shitty university nightclub called The Hothouse. Sticky floors and a smoke machine. Absolute comedy. And I remember that I ran out of songs to play! This was back in the vinyl days, the sort of thing where you had to just ***think on your feet, Jean***. "Everyone's pretty pissed," I thought, "So I'll just start playing the same songs again from the beginning." So I did that, and it worked out ok, you know? Wasn't a big deal. But my next gig—oh, you better *believe* I did my homework. And that's the thing, right? When we get kicked in the arse a bit, it's almost like the universe, or experience, is deliberately giving us a message. It's learning. And that kind of learning is potent, right? And you work to create it, so that you can, ***Jean, feel powerful***, because you know that you've *really* done your homework. It's important to hold on to the knowledge that you will be good at your job. That's the important thing to focus on. That's what counts. That's what *they want, Jean*."

A good stock of anecdotes is a wonderful addition to your toolbox, and collecting anecdotes happens naturally if you are interested in the people you are coaching.

Anecdotes can also be elicited from your client. We'll talk more about eliciting soon but for now, here are five questions I sometimes use to draw out a story from a client:

What's the toughest situation you've ever been in?

What's the most useful piece of feedback you've ever received?

What's the kindest thing you've done for someone else?

When have you exceeded your own expectations with a task or goal?

When have you felt really valued?

Technique: Use bigger picture

"This interview is a test. I must pass it."

"Everything is riding on this interview."

"An interview is pass or fail. It's a zero-sum game."

"Management is about winning."

"Effective management means telling people exactly what to do."

These quotations represent a limiting belief which one or more of my clients has held. Thoughts like this can trap a client. They focus relentlessly on one particular aspect of something, and this severely limits their ability to act effectively. They cannot see the wood for the trees.

Using the bigger picture is a method I employ to help a client whose focus is in an unhelpful spot. I use it most frequently to help change an outcome dependent mindset. When someone is going for an interview, and they are focused only on the outcome of that specific interview, for example.

To challenge this sort of thinking, I might say something like this:

"How many interviews do you think you'll have in your lifetime? Quite a few, certainly. And there's one thing that you need in an interview but nobody mentions it—luck! You can't control that, of course. You don't know what your interviewer had for breakfast or how they're feeling or whether they had an argument with their spouse that morning. You don't know if you remind them of their best friend from school or of someone who mugged them. You have no idea what state they'll be in, and you can't control it. So focus on what you *can* control. Do your homework. Bring your A Game. Be excited to be there! Nerves are fine. Nerves are your friend. Nerves tell the interviewer that you really want the job. When I'm interviewing people, if they're not nervous, then it makes me feel nervous!"

"Think of an interview like a rung on a ladder. Treat it like an experience. Don't worry about the outcome! Worry about it here, today, with me, and then worry about it afterwards. If you get rejected, then you have my permission to feel shit for one day. Eat your favourite food and watch crap TV. Whatever. Then pull yourself together and say, "What can I learn?" and focus on the next thing. You'll have lots of interviews in your life, and each one gets you closer to an offer."

"If you're a manager then you have to tell people what to do sometimes. Of course you do. That's part of the whole thing. You're absolutely right. The very best managers, of course, they see that they're part of a bigger goal, don't they? The have a sense of where the entire company is headed. They check in with their people. They *tell* them that they value them. They ask them if they need support. They pitch in themselves sometimes..."

When helping your client to think about the bigger picture, it can sometimes be helpful to ask them to draw things out on paper. If they have an issue with one particular colleague for example, then I might ask them to draw out that relationship first. I would then have them draw other relationships they have with different colleagues and perhaps estimate how much time they spend on each relationship. This exercise can help someone to recognize the panoramic view as well as the close-up. Analysis tools like S.W.O.T, P.E.S.T.L.E and S.T.E.E.P can help too.

Technique: Spatial casting

This is a fun technique. As I'm talking to a client, I will indicate a particular patch of space, and begin to associate that area with a particular character or feeling or idea. I often do this in pairs; putting a positive idea in one area and a negative idea in another. This sort of spatial anchoring creates a very useful shorthand for a session. It allows you to break the monotony of just talking and to communicate in a way which can feel deeper and purer for some clients. If you establish a spatial casting early, then you can refer back to it frequently throughout a session. When it's done properly, this can be a very elegant coaching tool.

Spatial casting happens unintentionally sometimes. If I am practicing a role-play with a client or doing a piece of coaching which may arouse strong negative feelings, I make sure to maintain an awareness of where my client is sitting. It's vital to control where someone sits or stands and what they begin to associate with that space. Move yourself or your client if it will help.

I was observing a coach while she ran a client through a series of practice exercises for a graduate assessment centre with the NHS. The session started well. She calibrated and demonstrated effective listening. Then she ran the role-play. She herself took on the role of a disgruntled consultant who is being told that their budget needs to be cut. She raged and shouted in character, doing a very convincing job. The client struggled to cope, and their state deteriorated. Eventually the coach ended the role-play and dived straight into feedback with her client.

"How do you think that went?" She asked brightly.

The client glared at her for a moment.

"Fucking awful," he replied.

The coach had made two errors here, or possibly three.

The first was in doing the role-play in the same seats as the coaching. The client still associated the coach with the difficult character she had been playing. Residual irritation and upset made the rest of the interaction much more challenging, and not in a useful way.

The second error was that the coach hadn't given the client enough time to process and reflect on the role-play. She tried to dive straight into feedback before the client was ready.

The third possible mistake that she made was that she didn't contract for the role-play explicitly. She needed to ask permission from the client, and to gain agreement on the terms of the role-play. This isn't always necessary, and might not have been if she had avoided the first and second errors. We will return to contracting in the Mokades Method.

"Do you want to practice the roleplay? Ok, the real thing is pretty rough. On a scale of one to ten, how hard do you want me to go on you?" Ok, remember that it's just practice today. It's just you and me so you can make as many mistakes as you want."

Technique: Props

I don't use props much, but I know some coaches who adore them. Anything can be a prop really, but some of the few things I do regularly use are teddy bears.

If a client is struggling to practice a future interaction, then teddy bears can help. Stay with me now. I promise they can. I assign them roles depending on the client's need. One might represent a loud, aggressive person, another an ally in a meeting, and so on. They soften the idea of whatever it is that the client may have to do.

For clients who are nervous about group assessment tasks, they can be especially helpful. Because they are more likely to provoke a smile than a frown, a client's fear of the task begins to retreat.

Technique: Role reversal

With this technique, I cast my client in the role of coach. I might do this loosely at the end of a session:

"So, I've got my interview tomorrow, tell me two things I need to do tonight, and one thing to remember during the session."

Or I might use it more explicitly, and amplify it by including some of the other techniques listed here.

"OK, let's try something. Swap places with me [**spatial casting**]. Now, you ask me the same interview question and let me give it back to you in the way that you just did. [I give the answer]. Now, tell me, what was missing? What can I try to do differently? [**eliciting**] Help me out."

This is a very potent technique. Teaching something is probably the best way to understand it deeply. In this sense, role reversal is a kind of advanced form of eliciting.

PITFALL WARNING: Please take care with this technique. If it's used carelessly then you can make a client feel out of their depth. They are not the coach—you are. If you ask them to pretend to coach you on something then you must be explicit about what you want them to do, and you had better be sure that they will feel comfortable about doing it. Role reversal should be a tool that empowers your client.

Technique: Proverbs

The more coaching I do, the more I recognize the value of economy.

The more you say, the less they get. The more you talk, the less they hear. If you can put it more shortly, more simply or more punchily, then it's more likely to get through.

Proverbs do this. They capture and distil a piece of wisdom into a flawless nugget of truth. Like this:

"Don't put all your eggs in one basket."

Just consider how else you might express that.

"Don't risk everything on the success of one venture."

That's not too bad, is it? But it doesn't stick, not really. Eggs and baskets—they paint pictures. And all in eight words, and nine syllables (by comparison, the second sentence has thirteen syllables).

This is part of why proverbs are such a potent learning tool. Sticking with hen-related ones for a moment:

"Don't count your chickens before they hatch."

Again, we could express this in a far more convoluted way.

"Don't make plans that depend on something good happening before you know that it has actually happened."

The word "chickens" paints a picture. The word "plans" does not. And again, we have the delightful brevity of this saying. This is simplicity that a child could understand. And that's the purest type of communication.

As well as strategic advice, proverbs are a wonderful source of philosophical truth. When I was growing up, my friend Patrick had a Nintendo. I didn't. It sucked. I wanted to be Patrick. I wanted his life, his room, his Nintendo. What I didn't realize at the time, was that Patrick had a pretty shitty family life. He had all the toys in the world because his dad was never around. And his mum, when she was around, drank. A lot.

"The grass is always greener on the other side."

When I first heard this, I thought of Patrick. This proverb encapsulated and articulated his situation, and how I felt about it, in a way that made perfect sense to me.

You can use any proverb that works for a client. Here are twenty-five of my favourites.

1. "A job worth doing is worth doing well."

2. "Actions speak louder than words."

3. "The flame that burns twice as bright burns half as long."

4. "Laughter is the antidote to existential pain."

5. "The slope contains many wonders not found at the summit."

6. "Absence makes the heart grow fonder."

7. "The squeaky wheel gets the grease."

8. "No man is an island."

9. "Fortune favours the bold."

10. "There's no such thing as a free lunch."

11. "If you're getting it for free, then you're the product."

12. "If you want to go fast, go alone. If you want to go far, go

together."

13. "If it ain't broke, don't fix it."

14. "Too many cooks spoil the broth."

15. "Easy come, easy go."

16. "There's no time like the present."

17. "Beauty is in the eye of the beholder."

18. "One man's trash is another man's treasure."

19. "Don't put all your eggs in one basket."

20. "The grass is always greener on the other side of the hill."

21. "Do unto others as you would have them do unto you."

22. "Absence makes the heart grow fonder."

23. "You can lead a horse to water, but you can't make him drink."

24. "Don't count your chickens before they hatch."

25. "Tell me who you walk with, and I'll tell you who you are."

I keep a list of these on the wall next to my desk and I use them frequently for workplace coaching and business coaching. If I am working with someone regularly, then a certain proverb can become a special part of our communication, a private shorthand which strengthens the rapport between us, and helps us to achieve our goals.

Technique: Insistent injunctions

I use these as a shorthand with clients too. Once established they can become a sort of shared mantra. They help with rapport too. I was once coaching a client called Crystal. She was perfectly warm and friendly when we spoke, but as soon as I began asking her interview questions, she became stiff and unsmiling. The effect was very off-putting.

At first, I tried to elicit the issue from her by asking questions. This wasn't working so I tried role reversal, casting her in the role of a coach. When she asked me an interview question, I responded with an exaggerated version of what she had done. She began giggling—she'd got it.

"You've got such a lovely, warm smile," I said, "don't be selfish—use it!"

It took a few more practice answers with me repeating this injunction insistently. By the third answer, I wasn't saying anything to her, I simply raised my eyebrows and open my eyes wide. By the end of the session, she had begun self-correcting. Together, we had managed to dissolve her unhelpfully formal "interview persona" by isolating the issue, making her aware of it, and giving frequent reminders of what to change.

Here are some other insistent injunctions that I like to use.

"Come on."

"Help me out here."

"You have a great voice/a lovely smile/deep experience—use it."

"Don't be selfish."

"I can only score you on what you say."

"Slow down! You're killing me here."

"Be generous."

There can be an element of theatricality to insistent injunctions, and this is something to embrace. If a client feels that you are really working for them then they are more likely to do the same for you.

Technique: Environment

We will discuss environment in a different sense later on, as it's an area which can impact a session profoundly. For the moment, I'm referring only to the things you can control in your immediate physical environment.

Many coaches prefer a neutral space; a kind of blank slate in which to work with a client. This usually means an empty meeting room with white walls, a table and chairs. Most of the **interview** and **business coaching** I do takes place in this environment.

I prefer a table which gives me the option to sit opposite a client or at ninety degrees to them. I find that sitting opposite is best for a mock interview style session. If the interaction is more discussion focused, or there are exercises which the client will do, then I prefer to sit at ninety degrees. I also require:

Pens and paper.

A flipchart.

Water.

I have other props available if I need them, but these are the essentials.

For **workplace coaching** however, and for sessions where I am seeing a participant more than once, I find it useful to deliberately create a particular environment, or occasionally, to go somewhere specific. This is deeply personal, and it varies from client to client. I have done coaching sessions in everywhere from a private dining room in a posh restaurant to a shisha café in Central London.

At my desk, where I do a lot of ad hoc coaching, I currently have the following:

A series of origami models. I make origami obsessively, and I sometimes fold a model with someone to help them change their state, or to illustrate a point.

Magnetic putty. This is an aid to concentration! For many of us, fiddling with something tactile is a healthy occupying physical activity which frees the mind. Try it!

Play-Doh. Fun. Tactile again. Allows me to set challenges for a client or help them to slide into a different state.

Dice.

Gold playing cards.

Neodymium magnetic balls. Tactile again and wonderful for playing or sculpting.

A frisbee.

Spikey light up balls, ping pong balls, blu tac, coloured pens and A3 sheets of paper.

Ten books filled with all sorts of wisdom, some of which I give to clients as gifts.

I also have various charts or illustrations which I can refer to. They include:

An MBTI type chart.

A learning pyramid.

A list of proverbs.

A diagram showing the best ways to communicate. (Face-to-face, then telephone, then email. I use this diagram constantly with new graduates that I hire.)

A colourful archery target with a series of goals on it. I keep spares of these and I sometimes hand them out to people as gifts.

A picture of Tolkien in his garden. It inspires me and sometimes I share stories about him with people.

Think carefully about your environment for each session. Most coaches have preferences in this area, and that's fine. The only thing I would advise is to experiment from time-to-time by trying a slightly different set-up.

Technique: Eliciting

Alongside listening, this is the most important technique for a coach. If you're serious about coaching, then you need to practice eliciting. It's essential if you want to be able to help a wide range of people.

To elicit – to evoke or draw out (a reaction, answer, or fact) from someone.

Instead of telling people things—which you should do rarely—you get *them* to tell *you* things. This is the magic bit of coaching. When it's used properly, eliciting is the most powerful technique that a coach can use to help a client.

I was working with Catherine, an executive in the music industry. She began by listing many reasons why she was unhappy in her career. At first, I listened. Then I began to ask her questions. Eventually, I asked her what she enjoyed.

"In my career?" she said.

"Overall," I replied, "in your life."

"Holidays," she replied.

"And how many holidays have you taken this year?"

"None."

"So, could you afford to take more holidays?"

"I could. But I'd need to reorganise some things."

"Well, shall we explore that?"

The question seemed to stun her. She stuttered a bit about the responsibility of her role, but we had a reached an important moment. After the session, Catherine began to reorganise her priorities around taking more holidays. A lot more holidays. She managed to go away eight times over the following year. Sometimes just for a weekend, sometimes for much longer. Eliciting was a vital part of helping Catherine. She had the resources to solve her own problem. I just asked her a question—in amongst lot of other questions—which allowed her to access that resource.

The more I manage to elicit in a session, the more effective I believe that session to be.

Sometimes, I fail. I cannot calibrate my approach correctly or I don't have the tools to flex enough to connect with my client to the point where I can elicit something from them. In that case, I resort to telling them things.

It rarely works as well.

Effective eliciting allows a client to really own a piece of understanding. Catherine owned her decision to take more holidays. It had come from her. It wasn't a suggestion from me. Jean owned her increased confidence, because she had decided to base her confidence more on her ability to do the job than on her appearance or some other quality. Tom started to listen because that skill aligned with the goal that he had set for himself.

Skilled coaches don't tell people what to do. They draw out answers from their clients.

To practice this technique, you need to frame things as questions. These will sometimes be very open, general questions:

"What are you hoping to get from this session?"

"How can I help today?"

"What's up?"

And sometimes, far more specific, closed questions:

[after practicing an interview question] "What is one specific thing that you did well in that answer?"

"Can you draw this out as a picture for me?"

"What are three specific pressures that you know your boss is under?"

Sometimes eliciting can feel like a game of charades. Like all games, people need positive reinforcement if they are going to feel engaged. For this reason, it's important to praise your client when they elicit successfully.

This is the essence of making your client do the work.

Part Two - The Mokades Method

This is the method I have refined over my coaching career. It is designed to deliver the most impactful session in the most economical way. I use this method for **interview** and **business coaching**. There are eight steps.

1. Build rapport (continues through all steps)
2. Calibrate (continues through all steps)
3. Flex (continues through all steps)
4. Contract (includes summarizing)
5. Work
6. Agree actions
7. Check buy-in
8. Close

I have explained the first three steps already. All I would add here is that these actions continue (usually to lesser extent) as the session progresses. You need to keep calibrating as you discover new things about your client. You must flex your approach when what you're doing isn't working. Rapport will build naturally as you move through the other steps.

The script below shows us points **one** to **four**.

"Hi, it's John, right? Good to meet you, John. I'm Daniel. [shake hands]. Let's have a seat over here, shall we? Just here. Great. Where have you come from today, mate? Super. Ok. Have a seat on this side, actually, otherwise it can be a bit distracting. Ok. Glass of water? Glass of water. [I fetch him one]. There we go, buddy. So, you have an interview, I believe? How marvellous. Well done. And it is with [name of organisation]. Right, and this is for the graduate programme, yes? Ok, super. So, have you had any interviews before? Tell me about them. I see. And when is this one? Tomorrow! Ok. Cool. So, have you done any preparation so far? Ok. And how can I help? What do you want to focus on today? Is there anything specific that you want to work on or practice? The competency questions, ok. Anything else? The group task, right. Ok. So those two things, yes? The competency questions and the group task? Fine. Which of those things do you want to work on first? The competency questions, ok. Now before we do some practice, are you familiar with competency questions? You are. Great. And how hard do you want me to push you during the session? It's just practice remember. An eight out of ten? Ok. Let's give it a go..."

Contract means agreeing the nature and direction of the session with the client. For **business coaching**, I also include a message about confidentiality. The key word here is *agree*. The parameters of behaviour and content must be set by both coach and client.

For **interview coaching**, firstly, I define and contract for the type of session my client needs:

1. A rigid mock interview with feedback at the end.
2. A loose mock session—pausing to give feedback at different points.
3. A discussion with little actual practice.

A rigid mock is most useful for someone who has never experienced an interview before. It's the closest to the real thing and the one that feels most like practice to some clients. The pitfall here is in overloading your client with feedback at the end of the session. All coaches do this sometimes, but it's something you must try to avoid.

A discussion is sometimes best for experienced clients; they know the game, and they may have firm ideas about which areas they want to work on.

A loose mock is my favoured approach because it allows for layered learning. In their first answer, my client rambles. I suggest a structure which they can adopt for their second answer. They use it, and they can notice the improvement and build on it *in the session*. These noticeable results can stack up throughout the interaction, so that a client leaves with a series of definite improvements.

Work

The next step is **work**. This is the meat of the session. It's where practice happens for **interviews,** or where you begin to delve into a client's particular needs for **business coaching**.

For a loose mock, I mainly use this structure:

1. Ask an interview question.
2. Ask follow-up questions. Probe.
3. Get feedback (elicit).
4. Give feedback.

Get feedback is pure eliciting. I ask a question to see how my client thinks they did. I might ask something general—"How do you think that went?"—but typically I will ask something much more specific. "Can you tell me one thing you did well in that answer? And what's one thing you need to improve on?"

My client's responses to these questions feed directly into my calibration. They dictate what I will do next—how I will flex. Common responses fall into several categories. I list these below, along with my most common actions.

Client's response	Coach's action
The client correctly identifies something they did well and something they need to improve	"Yes exactly!" "Well done, that's spot on" "I agree entirely" "Yep" "Absolutely right"

on.	
Client mis-identifies an area of weakness	"Anything else?" "I don't think so, actually" "My feedback is different" "I disagree—that was fine" "Hmmm...no, that was solid"
Client begins listing things they did well or could improve on	"Woah! I said *one* thing you need to improve on and one thing you did well" "Just one! Just one of each, please" "Ok great—but that's a list. What's the most important thing to focus on?"
Client mis-identifies something they did well	"No, that's not right" "No mate, honestly" "That actually wasn't good" "From where I'm sitting that wasn't strong—can you think why I might say that?"
Client struggles to identify a strength	"Come on—think carefully now, at what point were you really answering my question?" "Try again" "Anything else, any idea?"
Client struggles to identify a weakness	Use role reversal. Exaggerate the answer to highlight the weakness. Then try to elicit again.
Client cannot identify a strength or weakness	Check your calibration. Ask the question in a different way. Give hints. Use role reversal. Refer to earlier answers they have given. Use insistent injunctions—client may feel apprehensive about giving self-feedback.
Client still cannot identify a strength or weakness	Check understanding. Check phrasing—are you asking the question in a way which is easy to comprehend? Tell them.

By following this pattern with a client, we can begin to identify trends.

We can uncover strengths—and give lots of praise and encouragement for them. We can pick out areas for improvement, and give the client a clear sense of what they need to work on.

For **interview coaching**, I have listed below the most common trends that I see in my clients, along with the corresponding follow up actions that I find most useful.

Client does not answer the question that has been asked.	Elicit the trend. Advise them to repeat the question when it is asked, or to ask their interviewer to repeat it. Advise them to use the language of the question in their answer to ensure that they stay close to it.
Client gives a formulaic, pre-prepared answer.	Elicit the trend. This sometimes requires role reversal. A client will usually do this when they believe that it is unprofessional to speak naturally in an interview. Try to collapse this concept of professionalism—it is usually bound up with a mindset that an interview is like a test. "You must be natural. An interview isn't a conversation exactly but it's not an exam either" "Let me ask you the question again—this time, just answer in your own words. Imagine it's just you and me talking. How did that feel? Much better, right!? Do that. Be natural."
Client rambles	Elicit the trend. Elicit the concept of structure. I sometimes ask a client to pull a book off a shelf and compare a block of text with paragraphs. Which is easier to digest? Use the Sliced Bread method.
Client gives an	Elicit the trend. "What do you need to do some

answer which lacks knowledge	homework on?" "Listen—you gotta know your stuff. You just have to." "Do your research, pal. Don't throw this away." "You have time, and you have the internet—use it!" "If only there was some kind of global resource that contained all human knowledge and experience and you could access it from a device in your pocket..." [careful with the last one! It's supposed to be playful, not unkind]
Client trails off, stumbles or loses focus during an answer. They may stop themselves.	"It's ok, take your time" "It's fine, mate. Remember—we're just practicing" "Pause for a moment. Just gather your thoughts" Use Sip of Water technique. Use Arrow of Attention.
Client gives an answer which is too long.	Elicit trend. Elicit concept of structure. Use Headlines method. Use Rule of Three method. Explain C-A-R. Advise them to use the language of the question in their answer to ensure that they stay close to it.
Client gives an answer which is insufficiently detailed.	Elicit trend. Use Knight, Princess, Dragon. Use C-A-R. "Remember, I can only score you on what you say" "Be generous!" "Don't be shy—tell me exactly what you did" use eliciting statement— "Remember, it's not just *what* you did, it's also...[how you did it]"
Client gives an answer which is too short.	Elicit trend. "Remember, I can only score you on what you say—give more detail!" "Be generous!" "Don't be shy—tell me exactly what you did"

Finishing work

Most **business coaching** takes place in hour long blocks, so there is a natural rhythm to a session. In such cases, I typically end the work part of a session at around the fifty-minute mark. **Workplace coaching** is similar. **Self-coaching** should be short; twenty minutes or so.

When to end the work part of an **interview coaching** session is a more complex matter. I have run sessions that lasted fifteen minutes and ones that lasted five hours and included lots of practice exercises. I usually try to find a balance between giving my client a chance to practice, and generating some feedback that has utility.

In general, however, my sessions tend towards brevity—thirty to sixty minutes. I try to limit the volume of feedback that I give. Each piece of feedback that I give dilutes the feedback that has gone before. "Smile more" is a much easier piece of feedback to remember (and therefore to act on), than "smile more, and make sure that you use a clear structure in your competency answers, and research exactly what the training programme includes and make sure you give a firm handshake and practice your 'why' answer too."

When it comes to feedback, elicit first, then keep it brief and simple.

Agree actions

After the work of the session itself is completed, the next step is to **agree actions**. For this, think of homework. Useful questions include, "What key points do you want to remember from this session?" "Which two things do you need to go away and do now?" "So, what's the plan for the real thing?" I often use Role Reversal during this part of a session. It allows us to end the interaction with the client feeling powerful and confident about their future activities.

The actions you agree must be elicited from the client. If they state their actions, they will own them, and they're more likely to follow through with them.

The actions your client selects are their own, but it's a coach's job to limit the amount of actions that a client undertakes. It's also good to challenge your client if their goals are muddy or too broad. Actions should be as specific as possible, realistic, and include a time-frame in which they will be completed.

Actions vary from client to client, but here are some of the more common examples which I have elicited recently.

"I'll record myself answering three practice questions on my phone. Listen back. Make sure I am giving sufficient detail on not just what I did but *how* I did it."

"I'll research a particular deal that the law firm have been involved in. I'll find some specific figures to illustrate my knowledge. I won't just do skin-deep research. I'll check a load of different sources."

"I'll check the business section of BBC News. I'll follow up with more research on at least two of the stories that I find there. I'll know figures, not just facts."

"I'm going to learn more about company X" [too vague—challenge from the coach]. "OK, I will check their annual report and find some figures on them and their competitors. I will get a clear picture of the market and who the three biggest players are. I will find two developing trends in the industry and be ready to talk about them."

"I will remember the Arrow of Attention and to keep my focus on the interviewers and what they are saying. I will stick up the picture that I drew on the wall of my room."

Check buy-in, and close

The next step is to check buy-in. I do this by asking a question like, "Has this been useful?" Remember, a coaching session is useful only if the client finds it useful. This shifts naturally into my close.

"Thank you so much for this. I really hope it helps. Well done for today. Let me know how you get on [in the real thing]."

I shake hands and show my client out. Sometimes a close involves a follow up over email; a link to an article I mentioned or a video that my client might find useful. Sometimes (more commonly for **business coaching**), I will elicit an email follow up from my client. This might be a short list of actions that we agreed in the session, or a piece of homework—a plan or a piece of creative work that they have agreed to send me, for example.

Reflection

After a coaching session, it's good to take time to reflect on how you did. Just as if you were eliciting feedback from a client, try to limit your own **self-coaching** to one or two distinct pieces of feedback. Typical pieces of feedback I have given myself include:

"I spoke too much. I will try to be more succinct next time."

"I felt a bit distracted during the early part of that session. If I feel that way in the future, I'll start the session a few minutes late and use that time to try and steady myself first."

"Having my client draw out their response on paper worked well. I will add that to my toolbox and use it again."

In addition to reflecting by yourself, please be brave and let someone observe you. Another coach is good but anyone whose judgement you trust can provide insight or feedback that you might have missed. For observations, make sure to contract carefully with your observer and with your client in advance.

Part Three - Resources

The next section contains a some of the most common techniques and methods that I use to help a client achieve results. I have refined some of these methods over a decade or more and I hope that you will be able to make good use of them. Almost all of these methods came about organically; I have rarely attempted to design a specific method to help with a known issue. They were formed in a mixture of circumstances and through my own personal experience.

The things I have studied or practiced most which have helped me are reading widely, teaching English and improvisation, directing actors on stage or for the screen, teaching and making origami and djing. What are your own experiences? What richness do they contain? Are you making the most of their potential in your coaching work?

As with all techniques, treat these resources as starting points and be brave about messing around with them and trying out different permutations to help your clients achieve their best result.

The arrow of attention

This technique is best used with a client suffering from unhelpful internal monologue. As they are in an **interview** situation their attention turns inward. They begin to assess their performance and their behaviour. Their focus shifts away from their interviewers and onto themselves. They stutter, mumble and trail off in their answers.

When someone says they are nervous about an interview, what causes that feeling? Is it a fear of failure? Is it a fear of success (which is really a fear of delayed failure)?

Is it something else?

Changing internal thinking is far more powerful and effective than changing external behaviours. While the two systems are really one, helping a client to change their internal thinking habits is more likely to help them to shift their external behaviour.

Imagine that my client is showing signs of nervousness; stuttering, rapid blinking, speaking too fast.

How might I handle this?

I could say *slow down.*

That's telling, and it's not very effective. I could also try to delve deeper and find the root of the problem.

The Arrow Of Attention can help with this. When a client is nervous in an interview situation, it's usually because their attention is in the wrong place. It's focused on them rather than on their interviewers.

I first illustrate this through some careful eliciting. I draw three stick figures. One represents my client. The other two represent the two interviewers. When I draw the interviewers in this first picture, they will have a straight line for their mouths. My client will have an undulating curve for a mouth. This represents their uncertainty or nervousness.

"So here's you, feeling a bit nervous. Here are your interviewers. Now, imagine that your attention is an arrow. During an interview where is that arrow pointing?"

At this point, I may need to offer some additional prompting to elicit the answer I need. "Is it pointing at your interviewers?" usually does the trick.

"Exactly, it comes out of your mind, like this (I draw the arrow), and then it curves back...to point at you!"

I try to elicit the drawing of this arrow.

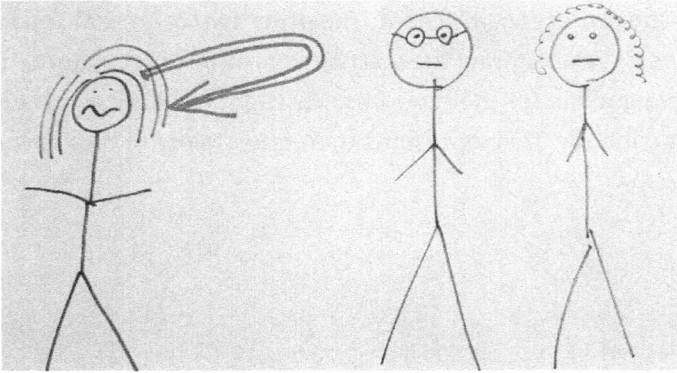

"Now, let me ask you a question. Are you a selfish person? I didn't think so. How much money do you think it has cost them to bring you to this point in the assessment process? And now these two well-paid people will spend an hour with you trying to get to know you, trying to figure out if you could help them to do a better job, and you're going to spend the time focusing on yourself?! That's crazy. And that's selfish. Why would you do that? You're not a selfish person. You just told me so. And I believe you. So what the hell, dude? Think about it and draw me another picture. And this time, draw yourself with a smile. And show me where your attention will go in your next interview."

They draw the picture, ideally this time with a smile.

"Exactly! Spot on. And this is what I want you to remember. There is a time and a place to think about your interview performance. There absolutely is. Think about it before. Analyse it afterwards. But during the interview itself, where will your attention be pointing?"

"At my interviewers."

"Yes! Precisely. I couldn't agree more. And from time-to-time you might feel the arrow twitching or wandering and at that point you scrutinize your interviewer, or you ask them to repeat the question. You force your attention back onto them and their questions, yes?"

At this point, you may want to layer and strengthen the concept by helping your client to add flourishes to the idea.

"Right. What colour is your arrow? And what does it look like? Thin or fat? Two dimensional or three-dimensional? Great. Remember this picture, and keep your attention where it belongs during the interview."

Life stories

Here are some stories I like to share with my clients. They are all true. They happened to me (or I happened to them). I reflect on them still, and I continue to learn from them. What are your stories? What details make them true? What message could your client take from them?

Shane and the Bike

Where did you grow up? Nice area? I still live where I grew up, and the area is nice now. It's gentrified, you know? It wasn't when I was growing up though. It was pretty rough. Scary sometimes. Especially for a kid.

I was eleven and it was my birthday, and the thing I wanted more than anything was this bike. It was jet black and cool-looking and best of all it had these buttons on the side right near the handlebars. When you pressed them, it would make these sounds like a videogame. Like sirens and bombs and lasers. I could not *imagine* anything cooler. And I got it! My parents bought it for me. "Joy" doesn't come close. I was in heaven.

So, me and my friend Luke—his bike was okay, by the way, but not nearly as cool as mine—we went to the park. We rode around for a while and then we pulled up and I showed him the buttons. He was flabbergasted. I mean, you would be, right? So, I'm showing him the different sounds and then I hear, "Oi, lemme see your bike, yeah?" and I turn around and I almost shit myself. It's Shane. Shane is a big kid. Really big. And he's older. And he got expelled from my school. And he comes from a horrible background, and he's horrible. Horrible and scary. And big. Much bigger than me or Luke. And violent. I remember seeing him punch someone in school. Really punch them. And my gut is just churning. "Lemme see it, yeah?" he says, coming over and putting his hands on the saddle and the handlebars. And he starts tugging it away from me and I begin stuttering and I can feel tears in my eyes because I know he's going to steal it and then I hear, "STOP!" and it's the loudest "STOP!" I think I've ever heard. And I look over and my brother is walking towards us. My skinny brother, with his big fluffy hair and his NHS specs held together with a bit of tape where he broke them playing football.

He arrives, and he puts his hands on the bike, gripping the handlebars. "That's my brother's bike," he says, "you can't have it". Shane looks at him, and his eyes narrow. "I just want to see it, yeah? Just let me see it for a couple of minutes." My brother looks right back at him. His hands stay on the bike. "You've seen it," he says. Shane sucks his teeth and leans forward. "I just want to *see* it, innit? Just a for a few moments, yeah?" He wrenches at the bike, but my brother wrenches back." "You mean you want to ride it—well, you can't. I'm saying no." "*He* said I can, innit?" Shane says, flicking his chin at me. "No," says my brother. "Come on, Daniel. Come on, Luke, we're going home." And with that he tugs the bike free and we follow him. Shane glares after us.

Now I have to explain something to you. Shane was big and scary and bigger—much bigger—than my brother. But my brother wouldn't back down. He was righteous, and fierce, and he stood up to him. And I'll never forget that. Never.

A Lesson Cheaply Learned

Stamps were the first thing that I got into. Comicbooks were the second. Now, you gotta understand, this is pre-Marvel Universe and all the movies, right? You had to be a goddamned *geek* to be into comics at this point. And I certainly was a geek.

So anyway, I started buying and selling, basically to build my own collection, and I found that I enjoyed it and I was good at it. I had a decent eye. I could find three copies of Uncanny X-Men 213, a key appearance of Wolverine with a great cover, and I could flog them for triple what I paid.

Not bad at all.

So, I started selling at comic fairs and through the mail. This is all pre-internet, right? And one day I get talking to this guy called Simon. And he's all, "Have you got this?" and "How about that?" and "I'll take two copies of that one" and it's superb. Very exciting. I start sending him stuff and he starts paying me. An issue here, an issue there. thirty quid. Fifty quid. Ninety quid. Super. Then one day he calls me up and he places a big order. And I mean BIG. Now I'm trying to stay cool but I'm fourteen years old and when I add this order up, it's five hundred quid. Five HUNDRED quid. That's, like three PlayStations or something. I'm in the money. I start thinking about what rare issues I might buy next. I draw up a list and dream about Amazing Fantasy #15 (first appearance of Spiderman) or a Hulk #181 (1st Wolverine). I'm drooling. So excited. So stoked. So, I package his order up nice and carefully and send it off.

Can you guess where this is going?

So a few weeks go by and I don't hear anything from Simon. I leave him a message. Don't hear anything back for another week. First hint of discomfort creeps in. I call him. Speak to him. Yep. Yep. Hundred per cent. On its way. Sure. Things have been crazy. Yep. Got them. fine. No probs. Great. Of course, he's been busy. Of course he has. He's a good guy though. Just needs to get it sorted. Yep. Fine.

Another week.

And so on.

Eventually he vanishes. I call his wife, who is now living with a new bloke. "He owe you money too, does he?" growls the new guy. I call his work next, where a nasal voice informs me that Simon "Is no longer employed here," and so on.

I never saw the money again. I never saw the comics again. I never saw Simon again.

Now five hundred quid at the age of fourteen is a lot of cash. But my word, I count that a valuable lesson. A lesson CHEAPLY learned.

The Shisha Business

So, end of university. No—wait. Final year—yes. I started a shisha business. I say a business, but it was basically me selling shishas in a bar. I worked *in* the bar but not *for* the bar, if you see what I mean. Anyhow, the owner was this lady called Emma. Very glamourous. I quite fancied her. Big old beehive hair and huge panda eyes. All smoky and cool, she was. And she knew me because I djed there sometimes. Anyway, I pitched the idea to her and she was up for it. So, I started selling shisha in the evenings. It went pretty well at first. We had a big feature in the local paper. There was no smoking ban then, so we sold quite a few. I was making a few bob. Not bad at all.

Are you waiting for the problem? 'cos you know there was a problem, right?

The problem was Matthew, Emma's brother. He wasn't a bad dude exactly, but he was a drunk and he was a bit of a lech too. In fact, now that I think about it, maybe he was a bad dude. I remember he used to clean his teeth in the bar sink and say awful stuff to the girls who worked there. Proper insalubrious character. Anyway, Matthew used to wind me up like you wouldn't believe, and me being a fragile, egotistical twenty-one year old, I wasn't very good at keeping my temper. One day I lost it and I called him a cunt in front of the entire staff. He was being a cunt, but you don't do that, do you? It was all pretty ugly. Then Emma rang up and shouted at me. Told me that Matthew was her brother and if he told me to do anything then I had to do it. He was in charge. How dare I talk to him like that? Told me to apologize or leave.

Now, I had sunk quite a bit of juice into this shisha thing, right? Basically, all my savings. It was my only source of income apart from djing. I needed to keep the money coming in, right? But I also wasn't having anyone treat me like shit. I was pretty determined about that. So, I stayed polite and calm when I spoke to Emma. I told her "I'll have all my stuff out of your bar within three hours". I called a mate, 'cos I couldn't drive, and he came and picked me up. I packed up absolutely everything and took it back to my flat. The next day I tore around town and I finally managed to set up a meeting with another bar owner. I showed him the product. He liked it. He said yes. "Great!" I said, "When can I start serving it?" I asked. He looked puzzled.

"When can you train the staff, you mean?" he said.

Something clicked. Finally. God, I was dumb.

"Train...the staff?" I stammered.

"Well, sure, you're not gonna serve them all yourself, are you?"

Within a month of leaving the original venue I had my shisha pipes in three different venues around the city. I was making more money in a single weekend than I had in an entire month at the original venue. I had more time to myself, and I had more time to expand to other cities, which I did.

You Moody Bastard

There is a short list of things that I don't enjoy doing. There is an even shorter list of things that I don't enjoy doing, but that I still end up doing—usually because of duty, loyalty or a very large sum of money.

One of the things I don't enjoy doing is giving speeches at the last minute, especially speeches on things which are not my passions. My brother called me, sick as a dog, and pleaded with me to cover a speech the next day. It was a thing about diversity for a load of business leaders. I wriggled and swore for a bit in my head, but I didn't hesitate. This was duty and loyalty. I said yes.

I scribbled some notes, practiced a bit, donned my suit and trotted down to central London.

When the speech started, I was nervous. I always am at the beginning, but I also know that I find my rhythm and calm down after about twenty seconds.

As I began speaking I noticed a guy in the front row, glaring at me.

He looked somewhere between pissed-off and miserable, and he was making me decidedly uncomfortable.

I tried to tune him out and focus on other people, but it wasn't easy. The guy kept glaring at me all the way through the speech. At last, I finished, and I did what I normally do—encouraged people to come and ask me questions afterwards if they wanted to. A few people came over and I spotted angry dude amongst them.

Shit.

I dealt with the smiley people first and then I was face-to-face with him. He had a sheen of sweat all over him. The bloke looked awful.

"I just want to say—that was fantastic. I've got the most awful cold and I was feeling horrendous this morning. I wasn't going to come but I'm so glad I did. I almost feel better now. Such a positive message. Thank you so much."

Glasses off

This is a very simple technique for anyone who needs to do a presentation or give a speech: tell them to take their glasses off. Having blurred faces instead of piercing eyes staring at you can help enormously with nerves. This is only useful for people who wear glasses or contact lenses, of course, though I suppose you could try wearing glasses that blur your vision.

Knight, princess, dragon

I usually try to elicit the second part of this exercise. It's most useful for helping clients to understand the nature of competency questions and how to answer the effectively. It can also be adapted for **workplace** or **business coaching** to illustrate the value of doing things which are hard. It goes something like this:

"So let me tell you a story, ok? And bear with me, 'cos this is a kids' story, but I hope it will make sense. Right. Imagine this; very many years ago, there was a beautiful princess, and she was locked up in a tower, yes?"

"Good. Right. So one day, a knight came along. Fine-looking chap; lovely horse, shiny armour, great haircut, ok?"

"Ok, and he unlocked the tower and let the princess out. And they lived happily ever after. The end."

"Now tell me—was that a good story? Satisfying? What do you think?"
[elicit a "no" from the client]

"Exactly! It was awful, wasn't it? My niece could tell you that wasn't a good story and she's three! So why wasn't it good? What was missing?"

[use spatial casting if necessary to elicit, like this...]

"So the knight is *here*, the princess is *here*. What's in between them? We need something there don't we?"

[to elicit further]

"We need a big, scary...what?"

[to elicit further]

"Fire-breathing...?"

"Dragon! Exactly. Now let me tell you the story again. Listen carefully, please. Many years ago, there was a beautiful princess, but she was locked up in a tower. So, one day, a very brave and valiant knight decided to rescue her. But to get to the tower he had to do battle with...**[elicit, then echo client's language]** a dragon! Yes, a huge dragon. Proper *Game of Thrones* style, with fiery breath and huge jaws. Deadly beyond belief. But this knight was super brave and very skilled with his sword and shield, so they fought for hours and the dragon wounded him, and he was battered and bleeding but then he finally managed to drive his blade into the dragon's heart and end the battle. And then, only then, after going through absolute hell, he arrived bloodied and battered at the tower to rescue the princess. And THEN they lived happily ever after. The end."

"So what do you reckon? Better story? Right. Exactly. *Because of the dragon*. You gotta have a dragon. Whatever the story is—you gotta have a dragon. Big or small, funny or scary—you gotta have one. That's the most important bit."

[for help with a competency answers]

"And that's what's missing from your answers. Stop skipping over the dragon! That's the best bit of the story! Tel me about the fight, the battle, the challenge. And tell me about the wounds you took, the cuts the bruises—the *adversity*."

[to amplify further]

Tell me, which knight would you rather have on your side in a fight, the guy who fought the dragon or the one who didn't? The one in the shiny armour or the one covered in bruises? Exactly! Be like him. Be generous. Tell me about your dragons. Remember—an interviewer can only score you on what you say."

C.A.R

C.A.R stands for **Context, Action, Result**. It's a straightforward and simple structure to help clients answer competency questions. I came up with it many years ago and have found it a very useful tool. Some clients will be familiar with S.T.A.R (situation, task, action, result) which is also good. I prefer C.A.R (it's shorter, and there isn't always a 'task' in a competency answer) but I will usually go with what my client prefers.

To teach this structure, I first outline the methodology behind competency questions. I will try to do this through eliciting. If necessary, I will first explain what competency questions are:

"Competency questions rely on a candidate being able to produce anecdotes. Each anecdote provides evidence of a particular skill or quality."

I will then try to elicit an example to check understanding:

"Let's say I want to find out if someone is resilient. If they can really deal with tough situations. If I just ask them in an interview, 'are you resilient?' what will they say? Exactly. They'll say 'yes'. So, what do I need to ask them? Yes. Quite right. I need to ask them for *a specific example* of a time when they've shown that resilience. That's a competency question right there."

"So, a good way to tackle this is with a clear structure. First you restate the question. Just give yourself a moment to pause and really think about what you've been asked. Reflect on it...*Give me an example of a time when you've shown resilience in a difficult situation*. Ok, now shuttle through some possibilities in your mind. The difficult customer you served that one time? The occasion when your event was undersold, and you only had a day to go? The time you got lost on that map-reading expedition?

"You want to go with that one, ok. So now, we have three parts to this. **Context**. That's the first bit. What does that mean? Tell me. [eliciting, role reversal]. Exactly. The situation you were in. And how long should this bit be? Do you think you get points for context? Quite right. Nice and short. Just enough for the interviewer to understand the situation."

"Next is **Action**. What's this all about? [elicit] Quite right. The actions you took. How important is this bit? [elicit] Yes. That's right. It's the meat in the burger. It's the most important bit. How many actions, do you think? [elicit] So perhaps three distinct ones, yes? And of course, it's not just about *what* you did, it's also about…[elicit] *how* you did it. Exactly.

[If you have used **Knight, Dragon, Princess**, then this is a good point to refer back to the dragon. In answers to competency questions, Clients frequently favour anecdotes with a stronger result over those where they were challenged more.]

"Good stuff. Now what's the last bit? **Result**. Yes. Now think carefully about this, how important is the result? How much time should you spend on it? More than context but much less than action. That's right."

A visualization can be helpful here. Sometimes I will ask my client to draw a car and underneath use a line to show the amount of time they should spend on each part of their answer. I try to elicit **10%** for **context**, **70%** for **action** and **20%** for **result**.

For the final part of this exercise, you may encourage your client to add another *R*. This stands for **reflection**. Useful practice questions to draw out this part of the answer might include:

"Reflecting on that experience now, what is one specific thing that you learned?"

"If you were in the same situation today, is there anything you would do differently?"

"What do you think you learned from the experience?"

C.A.R is good for structure, but it also helps clients to understand why a meaty answer—one with plenty of action[s] is so important.

Archery targets

This is a goal-setting technique. I recommend it primarily for **self-coaching** and **business coaching**.

List-making of any kind helps with achieving goals—using an archery target is simply a more visually emphatic version of this. I use a real archery target—the material is thick and will easily last for a year. The colours are bright, and I like the size of the thing—the dimensions are satisfying and noticeably different from A4. My own archery target sits above my desk at home, so it is in my line of sight consciously and subconsciously every day.

When it comes to the goals themselves, I work with a client to help them articulate exactly what it is that they want to achieve; "get promoted to MD", "finish writing new book" or "take a trip to Japan" are all well-formed, clearly expressed goals. "Do more running", "get better at writing code" or "feel more positive about my relationship with my boss" are not. Use the S.M.A.R.T[3] technique to help your client formulate a clear goal.

Once that is done, they can write their goals onto the archery target or write them onto a sticky note which they then put on there. When a goal is completed, it gets crossed off or taken down. Personally, I save the goals I have achieved in a year and look back over them near the end of December. This helps to reinforce the pattern of successful goal-setting over a longer period of time.

Over the last few years, I have also reduced the number of goals I have on my archery target to one at a time. This has allowed me to focus with great intensity on achieving one particular outcome at a time.

---

[3] Specific, measurable, attainable and agreed, relevant, time-framed.

The sliced bread method

When a client's answers, or their communication more broadly is long-winded or rambling, I find this technique helpful. I usually begin with some role reversal to try to elicit the issue. Then I ask them to draw a loaf of bread.

"Excellent. Now what kind of bread is that? A sour-dough seed loaf! Fantastic. Looks delicious. But there's a problem, isn't there? If I tried to eat that entire loaf at once, what would happen?"

"Yes! Exactly. I'd get sick. I just couldn't do it. It's too much to eat in one go. So, when you eat bread, what do you do? Right. Spot on. You slice it up. Then you can digest it, right? One slice at a time. Draw that out for me, please. Excellent. Now remember this image when you answer a question. One slice at a time."

Confidence number line

This is an NLP style exercise. I use it rarely and only when I feel my calibration with a client is particularly strong, as it can be tricky to use successfully. It's proven useful for clients dealing with difficult interactions in **business coaching** and for clients who get nervous at or before an **interview**.

Spatial casting (anchoring, for NLP) must be done sensitively and carefully throughout this exercise.

First, I select a space. I want a line on the floor, about a metre wide by four metres long. I want a natural space to start with, something we haven't used spatially so far in the session.

"Ok, let's try an exercise. Stand up, please. Now have a look at the carpet there. From this point to here. Now imagine there are numbers here, going from one to ten. Where is number one? And ten? Good. Ok. Now, I want you to imagine that each of those numbers represents your level of confidence. So, If you were feeling incredibly confident at this moment, you would go and stand on the number ten, got it? Great. Ok. Take a moment. Think about how you're feeling right now...which number best represents your level of confidence right now? Go and stand on it."

Most clients will choose a number around six. If it's higher, the session is probably going well. If lower, you may want to try some other exercise before coming back to this one.

The next stage is to elicit some of the associated feelings and behaviours for the level of confidence your client has selected.

"Ok, seven, yes? Great. Now how does that feel? Take a minute. Let's start with physical sensations. Can you describe your posture to me?

Your breathing? How does your body feel? Good, good. Now step out of the line and back into this neutral space with me. Ok. Now take a moment to clear your head. What colour is your front door? Blue. Right. And what's the tallest tree you've ever seen?" (distraction questions help the client reset to a more neutral state).

"Ok, now remember, this is just practice today. It's just you and me here, ok? [some reassurance is essential at this stage]. Good. Now, I want you to think about a specific time when your confidence was low. Take a moment and imagine it on one of those numbers. Have you got something? Which number is it? A three! Wow. Ok. Go and stand there, please."

Watch your client carefully as this new state sinks in. Watch their shoulders, their breathing, how they move...this gives you excellent clues as to how much they are invested in the exercise and how practiced they are at changing state. Remember that different people have different levels of emotional demonstrativeness. For some clients the change will be obvious. Others will "front up" trying to maintain a neutral façade even as their guts are churning.

"Ok. Now just take a moment to really put yourself back in that situation. How did it feel? What words come to mind? And your body? Your breathing? Ugh. Not nice. Ok. Step out, come back to this neutral spot. Phew. And breathe, breathe. Which way do the stripes on a tiger go? And what do cows make? And bees? How many colours in a rainbow again? Super. Alright."

[Make certain that you help the client to reset state after this step. It's essential for the rest of the exercise to work well.]

"Alright, now the fun bit. Take a moment and think about a time when you felt really, really confident. Oh, you've got one already! Are you sure? Great. Ok. Go and stand there. Wow. Just look at you there. I can see all kinds of differences. How do you feel? You mentioned your shoulders before, and your gut—describe the sensations now. Wow.

And what words do you associate with this number? Great. Super. Now come back to the neutral state. No rush. Ok. Super."

For some clients, this is enough. They understand the idea of creating their own state using past experience. For most however, you will need to complete one more step.

"Now for this final bit we're going to try changing your state. Go and stand in the number eight spot where you stood before. Great. Take a minute. Really feel it. Good. Now. Go down one number. That's a seven now. How does that feel? Now go down one more. Again, how does that feel? What is different from number eight? Ok. Now—deep breath! Walk down to number three again. Ugh. Can you *feel* the difference? Really feel it? Ok, back to the neutral spot, please."

Ask more state resetting questions at this point. Then elicit the ideal state.

"So, for this meeting you've got coming up, what level do you want to be at?"

At this point you may need to moderate your client's wish. We want relaxed solidity, rather than balls-to-the-wall confidence. It's easier for a client to move from a four to a six than from a four to an eight, especially if you aren't there to guide their state change. We want them to command a natural state of confidence rather than an exaggerated, theatrical version of it.

"A seven, then. Yes? Great. Sounds good. Ok. Start by stepping back into the three. Ok. Now take a minute. And then step up to the four. Yes. Now the five. Can you feel the increase? Good. Six. Now take a breath, then expel it and move finally into that seven state. Really feel it throughout yourself. Your breathing. Your posture. Your blink rate. From the tips of your toes to the top of your head. Really know what that feels like. And hold onto that state, and come back and sit down. Excellent. Well done. Have a sip of water. Well done."

This exercise usually ends with a brief discussion or possibly some recommendations. My typical summation might go like this.

"Now think about it, what's on the floor over there? The numbers were just imaginary. Nothing! Exactly! It's just a bit of carpet. So, if you can do this here then you can do it anywhere. Changing your state is about changing your internal thinking, right? And one of the easiest ways to do that is by thinking about how you visualize confidence. You said the word "tingly" to me at number eight. What a wonderful word! What a perfect description! And you can conjure up that feeling any time you need to simply by thinking back to this session, and by bringing up moments when you have felt that experience. What was the other word that came out? 'Prepared,' yes! So how can you feel prepared for this meeting you have coming up? Exactly! You need to know the facts before you go in there. Have a good sheaf of notes with all the detail that you'll need. And remember, you can control your own state. *You* are the boss of *it*. Yes? Well done."

Sip of water

The simplest technique in the book.

"Always say yes to a glass of water, sip and pause before you answer a tricky interview question."

Headlines

This exercise is similar to the Sliced Bread Method, but I usually employ it with clients who have a surfeit of detail or who lack structure in their communication.

I begin by eliciting the way in which news is presented; chunked down into simple messages.

I then challenge my client to do the same with their own piece of communication. I limit them to three main points.

That's enough for some clients. For others, you may need to delve into each point, asking follow-up questions to make sure that they don't fall back into unstructured rambling.

Rule of three

This is a fascinating bit of wisdom that not enough people know. In narrative communication, three of something is more engaging, satisfying and memorable than another number. Examples of this are everywhere, from advertising slogans to safety warnings to nursery tales.

With a client, I elicit the concept, then ask how they might harness it in their own communication. For **interview coaching**, it's most useful in competency answers (C.A.R, with three actions). In the **workplace**, I use it for training and knowledge retention with in-house systems and processes. For **business coaching**, it's a natural form for feedback to take; positive-negative-positive.

This is a very powerful communication technique and its applications are endless.

Put it in a box

Before I start a session, or at the beginning of it, I may notice that my client is distracted. Sometimes, I will try to work past this. As our interaction develops, the client's engagement may deepen and the distraction retreats. In other cases, I use this exercise. In my experience, it's best for **business coaching**; this seems to be when a client is most likely to arrive in a frazzled state, often having experienced some unexpected event before arriving.

I use an origami box for this exercise, and a pad of sticky notes.

"Ok, just before we start, let's try something. I want you to just take a moment and think about three things that might distract you during the session. Could be anything. Work, personal, a worry or something you must remember to do. Whatever. Write each one down on a separate sticky note. Then fold it up and put it in the box. These will be confidential. I won't read them, and neither will you. They can sit their quietly in that box, in the corner of the room, while we do our work. Then at the end you can have them back if you want them, yes?

At the end of the session, I offer my clients the chance to take their distractions back. So far, none have.

Tech tips

I am frequently surprised by how many people use technology in an inefficient way. I'm not talking about sending too many emails or checking you phone after work hours. I mean doing things the long way–manually reorganising something when there is a function which will do it for you, for example.

The phrase "there's an app for that" is smug and ubiquitous, but my word, if it can shave an hour off your day, do you really care? For anyone involved in repetitive tasks which use a computer, ask yourself this question: is there a faster way of doing this? If so, can I find it with relative ease? Sometimes, just asking someone, or the internet, for an answer will save you hours and hours of unnecessary labour. IT support people know this. So do developers. But very few other people who work in an office day-to-day seem to have this mindset. Help your client to adopt it with a few simple examples, from keyboard shortcuts to taking a picture of something instead of laboriously scanning it (it's the same technology).

As an equation, there are four variables:

Time taken to do the task the long way	= A (100 mins)
Time taken to find a quicker method	= B (25 mins)
Time taken to do the task using quicker method task)	= C (50 mins per
Average amount of times you do the task in a week	= D (10 times)
Total saving per week	= 475 mins

If C x D + B < A x D = then look for an easier way to do it!

Having your client draw this out for a specific task can be very helpful. This is most useful for **self-coaching** and **workplace** coaching.

Listen to yourself

Whether it's a speech, an answer to an interview question, or just thinking out loud, recording yourself and then listening back is a powerful learning tool. I encourage this mostly for **self-coaching** and **interview coaching**.

Counting down

Another simple technique. When you have a task, count down to the goal rather than up to it.

If your sales target is £100k in a given quarter, then begin with £100k on a whiteboard, then reduce the number as you make sales. If your target is ten hires by the end of the year then start crossing them off as people join. If you're exercising, count back from your repetitions rather than up to them.

For whatever reason, this technique helps with productivity and momentum. I recommend it for **business**, **workplace** and **self-coaching**.

Career graph

This is best used for **business coaching**, though it can be helpful in **workplace coaching** if you are helping a client to plot the next stage in their career.

Have your client draw a graph. On the X axis, ask them to note certain times in their career. Typically, this will be different jobs or roles that they have done. It could also mark high and low points in their work.

On the Y axis, in different colours, they can plot several lines. These might include any of the following:

- Earnings.
- Job satisfaction.
- Challenge.
- Opportunity for advancement.
- Work/life balance.

This technique can help a client to reflect on which parts of their career they have gotten the most out of, and where precisely they want to go in the future.

Time-shift

This can be a very powerful technique in the right circumstances. Instead of looking at something from the present, you encourage your client to examine it from their [imagined] future.

My client was Said, a successful sports producer who had been working in the Middle Eastern market for a decade. While he was excellent at his job, and had been promoted several times, he had become disillusioned with the work, and was considering a radical change.

After carefully examining different possibilities, he had settled on two viable options. Now, he was struggling to make a decision. Did he really want to abandon everything he had built so far? Would a radical change burn his bridges? What if it didn't work out?

"Let's look at this a different way," I said, "Imagine you are seventy. You're in decent health overall but your back hurts. You need to take pills for an ailment. You can't move quite like you used to. You can just feel mortality nipping at your heels. Now imagine yourself looking back to this point now. What would you say to your younger self? If I offered you a year in your thirties to try something completely different, would you take the risk?"

Said came to the realization that even if he took the jump into a new area and it didn't work out, *it still would have been worth doing*. He saw that he would regret not trying something novel—even if it failed— more than not trying it at all.

This is an elegant tool to help your client access their deepest desires. Use it with care and remember—decisions must come from them. This is best for **business**, **workplace** and **self-coaching**.

The memory palace

This is a technique which I recommend for **self-coaching**. You must practice this yourself if you plan to teach it to a client. At first, you will need somewhere quiet where you can comfortably close your eyes.

A memory palace is a location which you imagine in your mind. This will usually start out as a place you know well; the house you grew up in, your current dwelling, or a place you have visited many times and know well.

For the technique to work, you need to picture the place very clearly, moving through it and visiting specific locations in the same order (at first). You might visualize your front door first, then imagine yourself opening it and walking into your hallway. Next you might visit the living room, then the kitchen and so on.

You should visualize this *as if you are actually there*. Imagine walking through the location, and looking out through your own eyes. Practice a simple route a few times until it becomes smoother and easier. With each repetition, add a bit more detail—the more rich sensory detail you add, the better. Like this:

*"When I open the front door, I feel the **cool metal** of the doorknob. I see the **slick sheen** of the **blue paint** on my door and the light reflecting off it as it opens. In the hallway, I catch an **aroma** of sandalwood, and I feel the **weight of my steps** on the floor…"*

The point here is to really try and immerse yourself in the experience. Turn your senses inward. What can you see, smell, hear and feel? The richer and more vivid, the better.

Once you are able to access this location easily, then you can begin to add to it. At first, you may simply want to add more rooms. In time, you may want to add much more than that; furniture, objects, artworks, games, new locations or constructs and so on. And you are not constrained by money, or time, or even the physical laws of reality. If you want a green lightsabre sitting in a display case when you walk in, you can have one (imagine the *hum* of it! Feel the *glow*). If you want the Mona Lisa hanging on the wall, then grab an image from memory or the internet and imagine running your fingers over the picture, feeling the texture of ancient, cracked paint. Fancy that four poster bed from the hotel in Greece? Feel the weight of your body sinking into the mattress and it can be yours.

The possibilities are endless.

In each case, make sure that you explore the new location, or thing, with all your senses to really cement its presence. The more vivid you can make it, the more real it will become.

Once you have your memory palace, you can:

Use it to remember a list or a speech by placing memorable objects or things in a set order. This is sometimes called the journey method or the method of loci[4]. When most people refer to a memory palace, this is the main function that they are familiar with.

Use it as a mental relaxation tool. The exercise of going there and moving through each location in order is a wonderfully calming experience.

Use it to access more of your subconscious resources. This can help with difficult decisions or situations (see next section).

Have fun with it! In my own memory palace, I have a slow-motion water fountain, a pet tiger, a private nightclub featuring performances by

---

[4] There is a beautiful explanation of this, and other techniques for memorization in Derren Brown's *Tricks of the Mind*. You can also search online for a simple explanation of this elegant technique.

many of my favourite musical artists (living and dead), two pools, some top-of-the-range DJ equipment and every song I've ever wanted on vinyl, a gargantuan sequoia tree, a sunken jacuzzi in the living room and a delightful garden. The weather has been sunny for the last fifteen years except for one Christmas where I decide that it should snow heavily for a week. I enjoy messing around with the physics of the place too—I can fly. It really is fun.

The more frequently you access your own memory palace, the more you will find your own uses for it.

Getting help in the memory palace

Once your memory palace is well-established, there is a particular use for it which I have found very helpful. As well as objects and things, you can also summon up people. This works best if you know (or knew) them very well, but it works with anyone whose voice, image and mannerisms are familiar to you. Once the person is with you, you can ask them questions, getting advice and guidance on everything from work to relationships.

This is a peculiarly personal process, but my own system works like this. I have a dedicated room in my memory palace for these interactions. Inside, the lighting is low, and the temperature is a little cooler than elsewhere—this inner tweak to my thermoception helps me to think. I enter the room and sit down in a particular chair with a foot stool. I don't own the chair any more in reality, but it's very comfy nonetheless, and has become anchored to a sense of reflection and thoughtful consideration. Opposite me is a couch from my grandmother's house. It also ceased to exist many years ago. That is where my guest will sit.

I take a breath as I sit in the chair and bring my issue to the forefront of my mind. "Whose help do I want with this?" I wonder. My grandfather, long passed away but always full of solid, practical advice? Stephen Fry, with his planet-sized brain and deep humanity? JK Rowling and the brilliant, structured creativity she brings to our conversations? It all depends on the issue and my mood, but once I have settled on who I want, I call them. I hear a few noises as they emerge from the cupboard under the stairs. The tread of Stephen's feet on the floor are heavier than Joanne's of course. My grandfather walks more slowly. Then my visitor enters. Stephen Fry wears a soft green jacket. Jo's earrings twinkle when she moves her head. My grandfather smells of Old Spice. There are warm greetings. My visitor sits opposite me and asks, in their own way, how they can help, and so dialogue begins.

This technique is rather strange, of course—but it's rather beautiful, too. It may or may not work for you or your client. You will not know unless you try.

Part Four – The Tricky Stuff

My dad was a basketball coach for over thirty years. He coached everyone from primary school kids in wheelchairs to giants of the sport who played for England. One day I asked him who he liked to coach most.

"The ones who need it most," he said, "The people with no coordination. They're the ones who really struggle."

"But aren't they the hardest to coach?" I asked.

"Exactly," he said.

The concept of coaching mastery is embedded in this idea; that the more challenging the client and the circumstance, the more you can learn from your coaching interaction.

The final part of this book is about the tricky stuff; mistakes and errors of judgement, unfortunate events, tricky clients and head-scratching problems. It is necessarily brief; nothing teaches like experience, but I hope that this snapshot may help with some of your more problematic coaching situations.

Feedback can be a bitch

I was coaching a candidate for an intensive assessment centre with an energy company. I felt especially confident in this session since I had observed the actual assessment centre, and even advised on some of the content.

I was eager to get started, and soon after the candidate arrived, I was deep into an explanation of what to expect. I listed as much about the process as I legitimately could; what the assessors were looking for, what exercises to expect, and how my client might be scored on them. I wove in tips and tricks and techniques.

She wrote it all down dutifully.

We did a little actual practice—not much—and I ended the session. I was delighted that I had imparted so much information in only two and a half hours. A few weeks later, the client told me that she had passed the session. I was over the moon! I asked her for feedback.

She gave me some.

It was harsh.

She claimed that my information was useful, but that there was too much of it. She said that I had focused on the exercises and what to expect but there was nothing on the technical side of what the energy company did or what the role entailed in that sense. She criticised the lack of practice exercises.

At first, I was livid—I had spent two and half hours with this client and I was knackered by the end. And she had gotten in! Where was the gratitude?! The praise?

Eventually, I calmed down, and I began to reflect on her criticism. None of it was personal. All of it was legitimate. My knowledge *was* light on the technical stuff. I had spent most of the time telling her things (I hadn't learnt the value of eliciting then). I also hadn't calibrated effectively or built rapport. And there was too much of me talking and not enough of her doing.

It remains one of the hardest pieces of feedback I have ever received but it is also one of the most useful. It made me question my methods and adapt them. It made me learn.

Most tricky situations like this have something to teach us, and this perhaps, is the best advice that I can offer: reflect and learn. Embrace the difficult situation, do your best in the moment and then reflect and plan for the next time.

None of us can do more than that.

Difficult clients

Disclaimers aside, there are some clients who are genuinely difficult. The Mokades Method helps an awful lot with this by nipping it in the bud, or by modulating the session according to an individual's quirks and preferences. In particular, I want to emphasize the importance of the contracting step. If you have someone in front of you whom you suspect might be difficult then pay special attention to this step. You may even want [them] to write down in bullets the goals and parameters you have agreed for the session.

I would also emphasize the importance of taking care with spatial casting, and of getting permission before delivering a difficult message or engaging in a challenging role-play.

Despite precautions like this, you will still sometimes encounter resistance when coaching. This may manifest in crossed arms and eye-rolling or in an outright objection to an exercise or to your method itself. Below, I list some of the difficulties I have contended with in the past, along with a note on how I deal with them now.

Indifference

I have encountered this rarely, and only ever during **business coaching**. A common scenario is that a manager requests external coaching for someone they think is underperforming. The client does not necessarily want the coaching and has not requested it. They also may not understand what it is or how it might have value to them. This is a failure of management really, but the coach has to deal with the result.

When this has happened to me, I typically clarify what my role is to the client, and explain how they might make use of the session. I emphasize confidentiality to try and get them talking. Most people do enjoy talking about themselves, after all. This approach can lead softly into a coaching session. To mitigate against this indifference in the first place, I suggest you draft something for a manager to send or have a call or webinar with the client[s] you will actually be coaching to explain your role and the purpose of the session[s].

N.B – I was once coaching a group of engineers. I did three sessions with each of them over a period of about six months. My sense was that half of them found it useful, and half were indifferent. This turned out to be wrong. Individually, they told their managers that they had all found it useful and wanted to continue the sessions.

Sometimes you cannot tell if someone is actually indifferent, or just not that emotionally demonstrative.

Incongruence

In general parlance, this word has come to mean inconsistent or incompatible. In neuro-linguistic programming, it describes a situation where the external, verifiable behaviour of a person does not match what they say. For example:

[With crossed arms, looking down, monotone] "I'm really excited to be here."

Why does this matter in coaching? When you detect incongruence, it means that someone is being dishonest with themselves. This can be very challenging to work with. How can you help someone to achieve a goal that they don't really want to achieve?

An example may be helpful here. I was working with Sian, a client applying for a promotion. The more we spoke, the more she seemed to be trotting out stock phrases about why a management position was right for her. During a pause in the session, I asked her to tell me about a passion of hers. She began to talk about cooking, and her body language, her tone and her emotional demonstrativeness all changed. The energy with which she spoke was infectious. We switched back to discussing management and it reduced again. I reminded her that it was just me and her in the room, and that it was a confidential session. She took a breath and then her honest feelings came out: she felt that she *ought* to go for the promotion. It was more money, her peers would respect her more, and she believed she could do a good job. She didn't really *want it* though; it would mean less time with her family and a lot more stress.

Another example—which I have seen many times—is when a client is applying for a role in an industry due to cultural or parental pressure. "I don't *really* care about commercial law, but my dad wants me to be a lawyer."

Incongruence occurs on a spectrum, and each person is different. For some clients, part of your job as a coach is to help them to detect their own incongruence, and to do something about it. For others, it may be buried too deep for you to help effectively. You need to draw the line somewhere, and for some clients, seeing a therapist or a counsellor, rather than a coach is what they really need.

Defensiveness

This can happen in any coaching interaction, but it's most frequent with **workplace coaching**, often during feedback. The line between management and coaching is sometimes a blurry one, and what may be appropriate for a manager to say may not for a coach, and vice versa. Consider this carefully before delving into a piece of workplace coaching. Examine your contracting. Ask yourself if this is a message *you* should be giving.

The rules around contracting and getting permission to deliver honest feedback matter enormously here. So does knowing the character of the person you are working with. In my experience, clients who are higher in trait openness and agreeability, for example, will usually be less likely to become defensive. Choosing your words carefully is vital. So is selecting the correct environment—usually a private place out of the area where most of the client's work happens. Remember that spatial casting can occur accidentally too.

The final tip I have depends on your own influence at work, but as far as possible I urge you to try and get some sort of message about taking feedback positively into your appraisal system, and into the culture of the organisation more broadly. If people know that others will receive honest criticism, as well as praise for their work, then they are more likely to accept their own dose of truth.

Hostility

Thankfully, this is exceptionally rare. I have only ever encountered it when role-plays have gone too far, or a coach has begun delivering critical feedback without proper contracting and rapport.

In a situation of real hostility, I suggest ending the interaction, and possibly starting again at a later date with a different coach. You could also radically shift your approach—change rooms, try to start afresh with a different exercise, that kind of thing. I have also had success with defusing hostility by very carefully engaging with it; asking my client which of my words got them hot and then investigating why or apologizing. We all make mistakes when we are speaking and sometimes this can be enough.

Take great care if you encounter a client who is hostile or who *becomes* hostile. Remember; you never know what else is going on in their life.

A coach for hire

"There are two problems with Michael. One is that he pushes back too much. Every time I give him a piece of work, he comes back with a reason not to do it, or he questions something about it. The other is that he sends way too many emails. I wish he'd just get up and talk to people. It would be so much more efficient. That's what he needs coaching for. That's what I need you to fix."

This is tricky, because Michael's assessment of his own abilities may not match up with what his boss thinks. If you take on a piece of work like this—and only you can judge whether or not to do so—then setting expectations is essential, both with the person you are coaching and with the individual or organisation that is paying you.

In advance of a single session, a good coach will explain two things:

- What they do.
- *How* they do it—length and location of a session, coaching methodology etc.

They should also agree one thing in particular; the outcomes that the person paying the bill wants to see. How will success be measured? What metrics will be used? And when will this measurement be taken?

Be prudent about setting expectations in this way and you will avoid a slew of problems.

Coaching from afar

Coaching by phone or by video conference presents its own challenges. Briefly:

- The information you receive from your client which helps you to calibrate (and therefore to flex) is massively reduced.
- You cannot control the coaching environment in the same way as if it was a face-to-face session.
- There may be technical problems.
- You have fewer coaching tools that you can use.
- The overall chance of distractions is higher.

Despite these factors, I have frequently found myself coaching over the phone, either through video or audio only. One thing that can help is to add a little to your contracting step or to make your expectations clear in advance. I usually give these three messages to my client:

- Please find a quiet space where you definitely won't be disturbed.
- Make sure your internet or phone connection is reliable.
- Focus carefully on the session.

During the session itself, you need to work harder to calibrate, and your listening needs to nudge up a level. This is easier said than done, but with practice it gets easier.

One final note is to remember the *value* of being able to coach in this way. You can coach someone at short notice, help with issues which are current, and nobody has to travel. I've done a good deal of **business coaching** this way, and it has worked well, especially if I already know, and have previously met, my client.

Conflict of interest

This is most likely to happen in **workplace coaching**, but can occur in any coaching interaction. Some years ago, I was running a coaching programme for a large public sector organisation. One of the clients I worked with made several sexist comments during the session, in particular following a role-play where he had to interact with a female role-player.

This left me with a difficult decision; should I ignore what he had said, or should I tell the organisation that was paying me? Should I trust in their own workplace systems to uncover this belief? As distasteful as I found it, was it even relevant if the client behaved properly at work? Actions in a role-play might not mirror actions in real life.

What would you have done?

The best advice I can give here takes us back again to setting expectations and to careful contracting—if your session is confidential then it must remain so.

When it comes to **workplace coaching**, think carefully about what work you take on, especially if you have a prior or existing relationship with a potential client. Sometimes, it's easier—and healthier—for an external coach to come in and deliver a session. They bring fresh eyes and a fresh perspective, and sometimes it's easier to work with a stranger than with someone you already know.

Coaching in a disruptive environment

Is a bad idea.

Don't do it. Find a quiet place or don't do the session.

If it's too noisy, or it's not private or your client won't switch their phone off, then forget it. Good coaching needs investment from both parties. Your time would be better spent reading a book.

Everyone needs to draw a line somewhere. This is where you should draw yours.

A final thought

The path to coaching mastery is just that—a path. I don't believe you can ever actually arrive at a true mastery of this process. Even calling it a process diminishes its complexity. Coaching is about interaction, and interaction is a loop with limitless possibilities.

But that's ok.

That's what makes it fun and interesting, and sometimes invigorating and hugely rewarding. Things which are challenging help us to grow, and few tasks are as challenging as coaching people. I've learnt an immense amount from the time I have spent coaching, and I hope you will too. After all, machines cannot do this.

The more you keep an open mind, the more you read and watch, the more you act with bravery and try different approaches, and the more you reflect honestly and humbly on your experiences, the wider the range of people that you will be able to help.

The journey contains many wonders not found at the summit.

Printed in Great Britain
by Amazon